WHO, W

WHY DID THE
REFORMATION
HAPPEN?

CF4•K

DANIKA COOLEY

10 9 8 7 6 5 4 3 2 1
Copyright © Danika Cooley 2021
Paperback ISBN: 978-1-52710-652-9
ebook ISBN: 978-1-5271-0825-7

Published by
Christian Focus Publications,
Geanies House, Fearn, Tain, Ross-shire,
IV20 1TW, Scotland, U.K.
www.christianfocus.com
email: info@christianfocus.com

Printed and bound by Bell and Bain, Glasgow

MIX
Paper from
responsible sources
FSC® C007785

Cover design by James Amour
Illustrations by Martyn Smith

TABLE OF CONTENTS

THE AUTHOR

Danika Cooley and her husband, Ed, are committed to leading their children to life for the glory of God. Danika has a passion for equipping parents to teach the Bible and Christian history to their kids. She is the author of *Help Your Kids Learn and Love the Bible, When Lightning Struck!: The Story of Martin Luther, Wonderfully Made: God's Story of Life from Conception to Birth*, and the *Who, What, Why?* Series about the history of our faith. Danika's three-year Bible survey curriculum, Bible Road Trip™, is used by families around the world. Weekly, she encourages tens of thousands of parents to intentionally raise biblically literate children. Danika is a homeschool mother of four with a bachelor of arts degree from the University of Washington. Find her at ThinkingKidsBlog.org.

TO MORIAH AND
JOCELYN. MAY YOU
ALWAYS FIGHT FOR
GOD'S TRUTH.

THE FINDING
OF THE GOSPEL

Lost things, once they are forgotten, can be hard to find again. Have you ever cleaned the back corner of your closet, only to find something you once dearly loved? Maybe it was your favorite shirt and now you are too big to wear it.

Alas—that's a word which means oh no!—just over five hundred years ago, God's people lost his Word to

us. They didn't exactly lose the Bible. Instead, they lost the words in the Bible. Oh, they were right there on the page, but instead of reading God's words, his people wrote their own words—words that worshiped men instead of God. In the end, they lost the Good News of Jesus Christ. Common people—and even priests—no longer understood how to be saved from their sin—wrongdoing.

How was the gospel lost? You see, about 2,000 years ago in the early Church, each city-state had a bishop—a pastor who took care of the Church. After the fall of Rome in 476, the Church had five bishops, one for each large region. The regions were named for their biggest cities: Rome, Constantinople, Alexandria, Antioch, and Jerusalem. The three regions outside Europe fell to Muslim rule by the year 700.

POPE

In 1453, Constantinople was also conquered by Muslims. The bishop of Rome took the name pope. The pope became the leader of the Roman Catholic Church.

Our story of the Reformation happens in the Roman Catholic Church in western Europe. Things got really weird in 1215 during the Fourth Lateran Council. A council is a meeting of Church elders—cardinals, bishops, and the pope. Over time, the Church wrongly decided popes and cardinals had more authority than the Bible does. During the Fourth Lateran Council, Pope Innocent III presented lists of strange ideas, and

CARDINAL

ARCH BISHOP

the Church approved hundreds of them in just three days. They added human laws to the gospel of Jesus. That's bad news.

What kind of laws, you ask? Well, the pope declared himself Christ's one representative on earth. He also wanted the Church to control governments, and he made Jewish people wear yellow badges. The council said that during Communion the bread and wine turned into the actual body and blood of Jesus.

BISHOP

They said, too, people could only be saved through the Roman Catholic Church. Have you read the part of the Bible where Jesus says, "I am the way, the truth, and the life. The only way to the Father is through me."? It seems the council forgot salvation is through Jesus alone.

God's true gospel—his great plan for salvation—was lost a little at a time. The Church forgot to tell people the Good News of Jesus Christ. Not only did popes and councils decide they were more important than the Bible, the Church itself became corrupt—that

THE FIVE REGIONS OF THE CHURCH

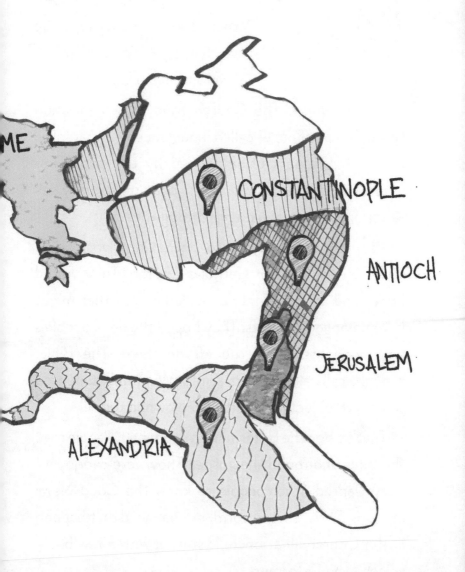

PRIEST

means they acted dishonestly. Important positions in the Church were bought and sold. The Church had two popes, then three, each trying to be in charge. Priests and popes lived sinfully. It was a mess.

It gets worse. The Church tried to sell salvation through slips of paper called indulgences—a guarantee of the forgiveness of sin signed by the pope. The Church sold indulgences, but it couldn't actually sell salvation. We are saved only through Jesus.

People began praying to dead Christians, called saints by the Roman Catholic Church. They visited bones and scraps of fabric—called relics—that might have belonged to saints. They hoped the dead people's past goodness would rub off on them. The Bible, though, calls all believers saints. We aren't supposed to pray to objects no matter who owned them.

That's when the Reformation happened. People read the Bible and found the gospel. They were overjoyed! They wanted other people to know the Good News of Jesus Christ too. Reform, or change, didn't happen in the Church all at once. It started with a few brave voices—the Reformers.

Why were they brave? Well, if the Roman Catholic Church didn't like what you had to say, they would pretend to take away your salvation. If that didn't work, they would tell everyone in the town you lived in they were losing their salvation, too—because of you. If you still weren't scared into silence, they'd declare you a heretic—someone who believes lies about God. That doesn't sound too bad until you find out heretics were burned at the stake. That's the reason even the people who found the gospel inside the Bible often didn't say anything. They were afraid.

In Ephesians 2:8-10, Paul writes: "For by grace you have been saved through faith. And this is not your own doing; it is the gift of God, not a result of works, so that no one may boast. For we are his workmanship, created in Christ Jesus for good works, which God prepared beforehand, that we should walk in them."

MONK   NUN

That's the whole reason the Reformation happened. The Good News of Jesus Christ was lost and then it was found. God's great plan for salvation gives believers in Jesus new, clean hearts and changes their lives. During the Reformation, the gospel also changed the Church, European governments, and then the world.

The Reformation took a long time—from 1350 to 1648—almost 300 years. The really amazing part of this story is what happened once people remembered how to be saved by Jesus. It's the story of the finding of the gospel.

FIVE SLOGANS FOR TRUTH

The Reformers invented sayings to help people easily remember important truths found in God's Word. The slogans each began with the Latin word 'sola', which means only or alone in English. The Roman Catholic Church used Latin—the language of Rome— to communicate so everyone in the Holy Roman Empire could understand each other no matter what language they spoke. The Reformers also used Latin to communicate with each other.

The Five Solas still remind us of the truth today, over 500 years later. God's Word alone (sola Scriptura) is our authority and tells us everything we need to know. We are saved in Christ alone (solus Christus) by grace alone (sola gratia) through faith alone (sola fide). All things bring glory to God alone (soli Deo gloria).

SOLA SCRIPTURA

Each of the Reformer's five slogans—the Solas—gives us a reason why the Reformation happened. Sola

Scriptura means Scripture alone. The Bible is enough for us to learn how to be saved from our sins and to follow Jesus. We don't need extra commands. God's Word is our authority—no man can add to or take away from God's instructions for salvation and godly living.

Before Johann Gutenberg invented the printing press in 1455, every copy of the Bible was handwritten by a worker called a scribe. That made each copy of God's Word expensive. Universities and monasteries often had a handwritten copy of the Bible chained to a table so it could be used by more than one person— and so no one would steal it.

Not only were Bibles in the Middle Ages rare, they were illegal. During the Synod of Toulouse in 1229, the Roman Catholic Church forbade non-priests to own or read God's Word. People were especially forbidden to read the Bible in their own language—all Bibles had

to be in Latin. The Church actually searched homes, and if they found a Bible, the house was destroyed.

The Roman Catholic Church told people Church officials were the only ones who could properly interpret

God's Word. They said the Bible should be obeyed, but they also thought the pope and councils could make decisions and speak for God. They believed the Bible plus their human ideas equaled truth. That led to some really strange rules in the Church. Not only were the rules weird, there were a lot of them.

The Reformation was the work of godly monks and priests. Scholars got involved, too. Why did Church reform start with priests and scholars? Well, they were the people who could legally read the Bible, and many had access to a copy. Inside the Word of God, these men found the gospel.

In fact, the Bible teaches us about itself. That matters because the Bible is God's Word to us. In fact, God teaches us how he feels about his Word right in Scripture in his own words. What does God tell us about the Bible?

In 2 Timothy 3:16-17 (ESV), Paul writes to Timothy: "But as for you, continue in what you have learned and have firmly believed, knowing from whom you learned it and how from childhood you have been acquainted with the sacred writings, which are able to make you wise for salvation through faith in Christ Jesus. All Scripture is breathed out by God and profitable for teaching, for reproof, for correction, and for training in righteousness, that the man of God may be complete, equipped for every good work."

There are important things you should know about the Bible—things the Reformers discovered as they studied Scripture.

The Bible is God-breathed. God the Holy Spirit inspired the writers of the Bible—ordinary men he chose as authors—to record the words he wants us to read. God let the authors of the Bible write his words in their own way, with their personalities and way of writing evident in each book. We can trust that every word in the Bible is true. God is always truthful, and his Word tells the truth too.

The Bible is infallible and inerrant. That means that it does not lie—and it cannot lie. Remember, the Bible is God's Word and God never, ever lies—he always tells the truth.

The Bible is sufficient which means enough. Everything you need to know about God the Father, God the Son—Jesus, God the Holy Spirit, and God's great plan for salvation is in the Bible. Scripture teaches us how to live for Jesus.

The Bible is clear. We can understand what it is saying to us. God wants us to know him through his Word, and to be saved from our sins by Jesus.

The Bible is our authority. It is the way God speaks to us, and we must obey it. There is no authority above the Bible—not the pope, not Church councils or elders, and not the government. All of God's words to us are in Scripture alone, and Scripture alone is our authority.

The Bible is also necessary. We need Scripture in order to learn who God is, to find out how to be saved, and to learn how to live. We need God's words to us in order to learn all about him.

Sola Scriptura reminds us that we must go to God's Word to hear from him.

The Reformation happened because godly men and women wanted to follow God instead of men. They wanted to hear the truth straight from God's Word in their own language. Christians wanted to own a copy of the Bible, and they wanted to be able to read and study it. While Roman Catholic popes were claiming they gave authority to the Bible, the Reformers reminded people any authority the Church had came from God—and from his Word. Once Reformers found the gospel in the Bible, once they read the words of God for themselves, they were willing to risk everything— even to die—for the truth of Scripture.

SENTENCES BY PETER LOMBARD (C. 1150)

Two hundred years before the Reformation began, Peter Lombard's 'Four Books of Sentences' changed the way people understood salvation by adding rules to God's gospel. Lombard decided there are seven sacraments—works—necessary in order to be saved.

Baptism and Communion are ways Jesus told us to show our faith in God after salvation. But, Lombard said they must be performed to earn God's favor before salvation. He also added five more sacraments.

Confirmation was a way for people to show they believed in Jesus. A priest prayed for people before  they died—the sacrament of extreme unction. Penance was a work assigned by a priest to show repentance for sins. Ordination was the ceremony to become a priest. Monks, nuns, and priests were forbidden by the Church to marry, but for the ordinary believer, marriage was also a sacrament.

FIRST STEPS
TOWARD TRUTH

God used many people to help reform his Church. Faithful Christians worked to help the Church return to Scripture for over 150 years before all of Europe heard about the finding of the gospel. Let's meet some of the early heroes.

JOHN WYCLIFFE (C. 1328-1384), ENGLAND

Wycliffe was a preacher and professor at Oxford University in England. He loved God's Word and thought everyone should be able to read it in their own language. He taught that the Bible says salvation is a gift of God—not something we can earn through good works. He also believed preaching should be from Scripture alone.

Wycliffe spoke against corruption and unbiblical worship in the Church. He translated the Bible into English and smuggled it to people through his followers, bare-footed priests who illegally preached God's Word to people in fields and streets. Because they could be heard softly quoting Scripture to the people they talked to, the priests were called Lollards, which meant mumblers.

Preaching from the Bible got Wycliffe into a lot of trouble. He lost his position at Oxford because of his teachings. Wycliffe stood trial often before Church councils and his writings were burned. He died before he could be declared a heretic. Decades after he died, though, Wycliffe was excommunicated—thrown out of the Church and his bones were burnt. That was supposed to keep him from salvation, but the Bible teaches no one can keep us from the love of Jesus once we are saved.

JAN HUS (C. 1369-1415), BOHEMIA

Jan Hus' name means "goose" in Czech, the language he spoke in Bohemia, which is now the Czech Republic. Hus was a priest to 3,000 people and a professor in Prague during the Great Western Schism when there were three popes—even though the Church claimed only one pope was chosen by God at a time. Schism is a fancy word people use when a church splits into two or more pieces. Hus noticed Jesus lived a simple life of love and service to others while popes and priests lived richly, sinning openly in many ways.

Like Wycliffe, Hus began to preach that the Bible alone is our authority and preachers should teach only from Scripture. Hus taught that forgiveness comes through Christ alone—not from the Church, the sacraments, good works, or the pope. He told his congregation and students that Jesus is the head of the Church. The pope is just a servant of God.

Hus was popular in Prague, but his teachings against Church corruption didn't make him popular with the Roman Catholic Church. In fact, one of the three popes had all of Prague excommunicated. The Church said no one in the whole city could be saved from their sin. Hus didn't believe this silliness, but for the sake of the people, he left Prague and preached to crowds in meadows and on highways. So, the Church threw Hus into a tiny dungeon, wrapped in chains for two and a half months. Jan Hus was burned at the stake while people joked about cooking his goose. His followers, though, remembered the gospel of Jesus and threw the Roman Catholic Church out of Prague. They formed the Unity of the Brethren church and taught the Good News to their children and neighbors.

GIROLAMO SAVONAROLA (1452-1498), ITALY

Italian monk Girolamo Savonarola was concerned about people living like Jesus. Savonarola lived in Florence, a city with lavish artwork, expensively clothed noble people, and monks and priests living lives of luxury and sin instead of serving others. Many of the riches of Florence came dishonestly through heavy taxes and embezzled money. Savonarola preached loudly about the sins of the people and called them to repent and follow Jesus.

For a while, the people of Florence were moved by Savonarola's warning to lead moral Christian lives. Maybe if he had preached the Good News of Jesus from the Bible, their changes would have been out of gratitude for Jesus' sacrifice for them. Instead, the people tried modest and humble living for a short time. In the market square, they built a giant bonfire and burned their worldly goods. Artwork, gowns, board games, novels, and toys all went into the fire. They called it the bonfire of the vanities.

The Church didn't appreciate Savonarola's bold preaching against corruption. The pope, like all Roman Catholic priests, was supposed to live a single, holy life without a wife or children. Pope Alexander VI, though, had several children. He certainly didn't like

29

Savonarola preaching about his sinful life. So, the year after his bonfire of the vanities, Girolamo Savonarola was burned at the stake in the same market square.

As Savonarola died, a fifteen-year-old Martin Luther was studying Latin in a German town a little over six hundred miles north. Earlier, in 1455, a man named Johann Gutenberg had invented a marvelous machine that printed Bibles quickly and accurately. Reform was coming, and no pope would be able to stop it.

NINETY-FIVE THESES BY MARTIN LUTHER (1517)

Near the church and university where the priest Martin Luther taught, the Church was selling plenary indulgences, a piece of paper that was supposed to guarantee forgiveness of all the purchaser's sins. Luther knew the Bible says only God can forgive sin. We must believe in Jesus to be saved by grace through faith.

Luther made a list of arguments against indulgences. He nailed his Ninety-Five Theses to the door of the Wittenberg Castle Church. Luther made statements like:

- The pope cannot forgive sins.

- God only forgives sinners who repent.

- People who buy indulgences might go to hell, because they believe in a piece of paper instead of Jesus.

The Ninety-Five Theses spread quickly across Europe. This short document was read by common people, priests, and even the pope. It was the spark that started the Reformation fire.

SOLUS CHRISTUS

Solus Christus, or solo Christo, is the slogan the Reformers used to remind us that Jesus is the only way to be saved from our sins. Jesus alone is our King and Lord. He is the only one we should worship, obey, and believe in. He alone is worthy of our praise. The Reformers wanted us to stay away from idolatry, false worship, and false messiahs.

Has anyone ever hurt you? Maybe they took something you cared about or they hit you. Did you want someone to make the wrong against you right?

We expect a judge to punish a person who hurts others. Our God is a just judge—that means he is fair and we can trust his decisions. He is also a good God—there is nothing bad or unfair in him. One day, God will judge every person who has ever lived. He will punish all sin. Now, sometimes people feel like they don't have any sin to judge. But the Bible tells us even the smallest lie or anger toward your mom or dad is sin that separates us from God forever. We've all sinned, and our sin deserves death—that is just.

But—and here's some really good news—God made a way for us to be with him forever. God the Father sent Jesus, God the Son, to be born as a human. Jesus lived a perfect and holy life.

Every one of us deserves to be judged for our wrongdoing, but Jesus took the judgment instead. He died in the place of the people he came to save. If we believe in Jesus and confess our belief out loud to others, we will be saved—our sins will be forgiven forever (Romans 10:9). Then God the Holy Spirit will live in our hearts. We will spend eternity with God. That's amazing, right?

The author of Hebrews writes all about Jesus and how amazing he is. In Hebrews 1:1-4, he says: "Long ago, at many times and in many ways, God spoke to our fathers by the prophets, but in these last days he has spoken to us by his Son, whom he appointed the heir of all things, through whom also he created the world. He is the radiance of the glory of God and the exact

imprint of his nature, and he upholds the universe by the word of his power. After making purification for sins, he sat down at the right hand of the Majesty on high, having become as much superior to angels as the name he has inherited is more excellent than theirs."

The Bible tells us a lot about Jesus, God the Son. Here are some important things we learn:

The Old Testament teaches there is one God. He is the only true God, the Creator of Heaven and Earth. He rules over heavenly creatures, the planets, kings and nations, and all people. There is a mystery that only God truly understands about himself: our one true God is three persons in one God. God the Father, God the Son, and God the Holy Spirit appear together in the Bible a number of times. They talk to each other and about each other. The word Trinity is not in the Bible, but it's the word we use to explain that there are three persons in one God.

Another mystery is that Jesus is truly God and truly man at the same time. Jesus never sinned. He is the only sinless human—because he is God. That is the reason he could take the punishment for the sins of his followers.

Jesus is the Messiah—the Savior—God tells us about through the prophets in the Old Testament. Jesus is the Way, the Truth and the Life. There is no other way to the Father except through Jesus.

Jesus is alive. He rose to life three days after his death. One day, he will return for his people and judge the sins of every person who has lived. Remember, if you belong to Jesus, he has already taken your punishment.

Jesus is our intercessor. That means he pleads our court case in front of God the Father. The Father adopts everyone who follows Jesus as his own child. Also, if you believe in and follow Jesus, he says you are no longer his servant. Instead he calls you his friend.

Jesus alone is the one who created us, loves us, and saves us from our sins. We don't need to add anything to God's great plan for our salvation. Jesus' perfect obedient life, his death in our place, and his resurrection from the dead are enough.

INSTITUTES OF CHRISTIAN RELIGION BY JOHN CALVIN (1536, 1539, 1559)

One of the most famous documents from the Reformation is John Calvin's systematic theology, Institutes of the Christian Religion. Theology means the study of God. Calvin spent over twenty years writing about God the Father, God the Son, God the Holy Spirit, and the Church. His first volume in 1536 was just six chapters long. By 1559, Calvin had expanded the Institutes to four books with a total of eighty chapters.

Calvin's work is well known for his biblical emphasis on God's sovereign rule as King of the Universe. We sinners are dead in our sins and cannot do anything to earn salvation. Instead, God chooses to make us alive in Jesus. It is a free gift, and God chose his people before the beginning of the earth. You can read Ephesians chapters 1 and 2 to learn more about what God says about salvation.

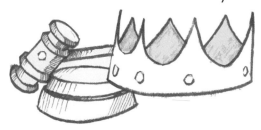

REFORMERS
REFORMING THINGS

While there were many men and women who contributed to the Reformation, these five changed the world.

MARTIN LUTHER (1483-1546), GERMANY

As a law student, Martin Luther was nearly killed by a lightning bolt. He became a monk after begging Saint Anna to spare his life. Luther denied himself food and sleep in an attempt to earn God's favor. He was shocked to read in the Bible that salvation is in Christ by grace through faith.

Luther's list of complaints against indulgences, the Ninety-Five Theses, kicked off a revolution that spread across the entire continent. The many books, pamphlets, and Bible commentaries Luther wrote are still studied today. He preached sola gratia loudly—we are saved by God's grace alone.

Because of his sola Scriptura teaching that the decrees of councils and popes cannot overthrow the clear teaching of the Bible, Luther stood trial multiple times. He was kidnapped, declared a heretic, excommunicated by the pope, and thrown out of his monastic order. He responded by translating the Bible into German, marrying a feisty nun, Katie, and caring for a big family.

ULRICH ZWINGLI (1484-1531), SWITZERLAND

The Reformation truly began in Switzerland during the "Affair of the Sausages." During the forty days before Easter, in which the Roman Catholic Church forbade people to eat meat, a group of men priest Ulrich Zwingli was dining with served sausage. Though Zwingli didn't eat any, he later preached a sermon called "On the Choice and Freedom of Foods." He said following Jesus was important—keeping the made-up rules of the Church was not.

Ulrich Zwingli loved Scripture and he preached from the Bible book-by-book. Zwingli took the idols of saints out of the churches in Zurich and focused worship on God's Word. A terrible bout of the Black Plague helped Zwingli learn about God's sovereignty—his kingly rule—and God's care for his people.

Zwingli and Luther argued over whether the bread and wine in Communion actually turn into Jesus' body and blood. That argument divided the newly created Protestant Church into Lutherans—who did believe the meal was really Jesus' body, and the Reformed Church—who agreed Communion is a symbolic way to remember Jesus' sacrifice.

JOHN CALVIN (1509-1564), FRANCE / SWITZERLAND

The same year God saved John Calvin in Jesus by grace through faith, Calvin's friend preached against Roman Catholic theologians. Accused of writing the sermon, Calvin escaped death by climbing through a window and

down a rope of bedsheets. He disguised himself as a farmer and settled in Geneva, Switzerland to lead the Reformation there.

Calvin is best known for his views on salvation, but he also worked hard to make sure people in the Church lived strict moral lives. In fact, Calvin wanted Geneva to be the kingdom of God here on earth. Each citizen had to sign a statement of faith, agreeing to live for Jesus. Some of the people who complained loudly were executed. That's pretty strict. Calvin believed that if you loved Jesus, your life would show it.

He lived strictly for Jesus himself, preaching three times a day. In addition to the famous Institutes of the Christian Religion, Calvin wrote a commentary on nearly every book of the Bible, devotions, and pamphlets explaining doctrine—beliefs outlined in Scripture.

THOMAS CRANMER (1489-1556), ENGLAND

Now here is an interesting story from history, parts of which may not be wholly true. King Henry VIII wanted a divorce. That is certainly true. Some people say Henry sent Cardinal Wolsey and his greyhound, Urian, to beg the pope to allow Henry's divorce. The story is that while Wolsey was kissing the pope's toe,

Urian bit the pope's foot and angered him. Whether Urian's role in Henry's request is true or not, the pope refused Henry's divorce. Thomas Cranmer was made Archbishop of Canterbury, and Cranmer gave Henry his divorce. Meanwhile, Henry became the supreme head of the Church of England and the Roman Catholic Church was kicked out of England.

When Henry's nine-year-old son, Edward VI, became king, Cranmer made kingly decisions for him. Cranmer brought Reformed professors from across

Europe to teach at the universities. Churches were stripped of their idols. Worship services focused on the Bible. People began to read Scripture daily and the poor, widowed, and orphaned were cared for.

Alas—so sad, Edward died just six years later, and his older sister Bloody Mary became queen. In five years, Mary burned over 300 Protestants at the stake, including Cranmer. Eight hundred Protestants ran for their lives. When Mary died, her sister Elizabeth allowed Protestants to worship freely. The Church of England became known as the Anglican Church in England and the Episcopal Church in America.

JOHN KNOX (C.1513-1572), SCOTLAND

John Knox was the bodyguard for Scottish Reformer George Wishart. When Wishart was murdered in 1546, Protestant rebels overtook St. Andrew's Castle and killed the Roman Catholic cardinal. They set up a Reformed community and made Knox their pastor.

After the French conquered the castle, Knox was sentenced to row as a slave on a galley ship. Rowing was devastatingly hard, and Knox nearly died. Even so, when he was forced to kiss a painting of Saint Mary, Knox hurled the picture into the sea, shouting, "Let her save herself!" He would not be a part of worshiping pictures, statues, or dead people—even if it meant his death.

Once he was freed from slavery, Knox spent many of his years in exile, traveling to Germany, on to Geneva—where he studied under Calvin twice, and then back to Scotland. Through Knox' leadership, all of Scotland became Protestant and the Presbyterian Church was born. Scotland became a place of freedom where the gospel was loudly proclaimed.

BOOK OF COMMON PRAYER BY THOMAS CRANMER (1549, 1552)

Thomas Cranmer believed that "God's worde written"—the Bible—changes lives. The people of England had been attending the Roman Catholic Mass in Latin. Cranmer wanted the priests and common people—for whom the book was named—to have a church service that would help them hear God's Word and pray in a way that would glorify God and teach them what the Bible says about him.

Cranmer created a book of prayers and a schedule for reading the Bible in church. Cranmer wrote his schedule of public Bible reading so that by reading each day, believers would hear the Old Testament once each year, the New Testament twice, and the Psalms were read through once per month. The Book of Common Prayer has been revised several times and is still used in Anglican churches throughout the world today.

SOLA GRATIA
AND SOLA FIDE

Now, you know all about God's justice. You know the punishment for sin is death, and that salvation comes only through Jesus who took the punishment for the sins of his followers. Believers in Jesus are saved.

You also know the medieval Roman Catholic Church taught that in order to be saved, people had to perform six of the seven sacraments. But that wasn't enough—even if someone was baptized, confirmed his faith, took Communion regularly, was prayed for by a priest when he was terribly sick, confessed his sins to a priest, and was either ordained as a priest or nun or married, that didn't mean that person was saved. In fact, the Church taught no one could really know if they were saved.

The Church also taught there is a place called purgatory where people go after they die to pay for their sins through extra punishment. Even a believer could be in purgatory for millions of years. After confessing sins to a priest, there was work to be done that would help reduce time in purgatory.

Penance was a special job assigned by the priest. It could include prayer, giving money, fasting, making a trip to see a place considered holy, or even whipping oneself. Indulgences were supposed to help people spend less time in purgatory, and plenary indulgences were purchased in the hope of skipping Purgatory all together.

Remember the Reformers' first sola? That's right. It is sola Scriptura—the Bible alone is our authority. If an instruction is not in God's Word, it isn't necessary for salvation. The Reformers were upset about the

teachings of the Church. You see, purgatory, penance, and indulgences are not in the Bible. Also, the Bible doesn't say elders in the Church can't be married—it actually says they should have just one wife. We know, too, that if we love Jesus, we are saved forever. No one can steal us from his love.

For centuries, the Roman Catholic priests and theologians taught a false gospel. But the Reformers found the true gospel of Jesus Christ, right there in the pages of Scripture. They wanted to make sure people heard only the truth, the whole truth, and nothing but the truth. So, how does one get saved?

Remember, the Bible tells us God is holy and perfect. God has never done anything wrong, and he never will. Every person, though, has sinned—they have broken God's laws. Because of our sin, we are separated from God. The payment for sin is death. That's bad news, right?

God loves us, though, and made a plan for our salvation. God the Father sent God the Son, Jesus, to live a perfect and holy life here on earth—truly God and truly man. Jesus paid for our sin with his own life when he took our punishment on himself—he was tortured and then crucified. Jesus gives his own righteousness to anyone who believes in him and confesses him out loud. Believers repent—turn back—of their sin and live their lives for Jesus.

God the Holy Spirit lives in the heart of each person who believes in Jesus and is saved. Saved from what? We are saved from God's wrath—the punishment we deserve from a just and holy God. Every believer will live forever with God. That's the Good News of Jesus Christ.

In Ephesians 2:8-9, we learn: "For by grace you have been saved through faith. And this is not your own doing; it is the gift of God, not a result of works, so that no one may boast."

What does it mean that we are saved by grace through faith?

Grace is a gift from God that we don't deserve. We did not earn God's love. We can't buy it. We can't believe enough, or work hard enough to earn it. In fact, we didn't even know we needed grace. God gives his children the free gift of his favor because he chooses to do so. That's what sola gratia means—by grace alone. We cannot be saved without God first pouring out his grace on us.

Sola fide means through faith alone. Faith means to trust. We are saved from our sin only when we trust in Jesus. We are not saved just by knowing the truth about Jesus. We also can't be saved accidentally or because our parents or grandparents are Christians. If you love Jesus and trust him to save you from your sins—then you have faith in him.

Romans 10:8-9 says, "But what does it say? "The word is near you, in your mouth and in your heart" (that is, the word of faith that we proclaim); because, if you confess with your mouth that Jesus is Lord and believe in your heart that God raised him from the dead, you will be saved."

That's it. If you believe God raised Jesus from the dead and confess with your mouth that Jesus is Lord, you will be forever saved and God will forgive your sins. Then, God will help you repent of your sins and live for Jesus. Amazing, isn't it?

The Reformers wanted us to remember that salvation is all about what Jesus did for us. We are saved by God's grace through the faith he gives us. Sola gratia and sola fide!

ACTS AND MONUMENTS BY JOHN FOXE (1563)

John Foxe (1516-1587) was saved by Jesus in England. Persecuted for his Reformed beliefs, he and his wife hid in the homes of kind people until Queen Mary's reign when they fled to the Netherlands, Germany, and finally Switzerland. As they traveled, Foxe witnessed people killed for their faith. He recorded their stories. When Reformed believers throughout Europe heard about his work, they sent Foxe their own stories of persecution and martyrdom.

Ecclesiastical History, Contayning the Actes and Monuments of Things Passed In Every Kynges Tyme is a long title. The original title was much longer— fifty-six words to be exact. It was shortened simply to Foxe's Book of Martyrs. Foxe's book tells the story of Christian martyrs from Stephen and the apostles all the way through Thomas Cranmer. Over the centuries, authors have added more stories, shortened the history, and translated Foxe's Book into modern English.

MORE
REFORMERS REFORMING

God works in and through the lives of his people to grow their character and to bring glory to himself. The time of the Reformation was no different. You've met the main pastors leading the Reformation, but there were many men and women working tirelessly to further the Good News of Jesus Christ.

WILLIAM TYNDALE (1494-1536), ENGLAND

John Wycliffe was the first person to translate the Bible into English. By the time William Tyndale was born 112 years later, the English language had changed drastically. This is how Wycliffe translated John 3:16: "For God louede so the world, that he af his oon bigetun sone, that ech man that bileueth in him perische not, but haue euerlastynge lijf." It's a little hard to read today.

It was still illegal to translate the Bible into English, but Tyndale was determined to see even farmer boys be able to read God's Word in their own language. He

spent twelve years on the run in Europe, translating the Bible. Tyndale's printed English Bible was smuggled into England. King Henry VIII had Tyndale strangled and his body burned at the stake. Even so, Tyndale's translation is still being used today. Over eight out of every ten words in the King James Bible were translated and arranged by Tyndale.

PHILIP MELANCHTHON (1497-1560), GERMANY

A friend and colleague of Martin Luther, Philip Melanchthon was a brilliant professor. Melanchthon was committed to unity and wanted the Lutheran and Reformed Churches to agree with each other. His willingness to compromise in order to help Christians serve Jesus was sometimes alarming to Luther, but Melanchthon's gentle spirit and well-reasoned arguments helped win people to the reforming movement of the Church.

Melanchthon wrote the Augsburg Confession, which explained the beliefs of the Lutheran Church. After Luther's death, he altered the confession and removed the emphasis on the idea that during Communion the bread and wine become Jesus' actual body and blood. This new version, the Variata, was a confession of faith both Lutheran and Reformed believers could fully agree with.

KATHARINA ZELL (1497-1562), GERMANY

Katharina married former priest and Reformer Matthew Zell and spent her life caring for others. Not only did Katharina visit prisons and hospitals, she also fed and sheltered thousands of refugees during the religious wars and persecutions of the Reformation. One night the Zells had eighty people in their home— sixty of them stayed for almost a month. Reformers also stayed with the Zells, like John Calvin and Ulrich Zwingli.

Katharina was an author. She wrote Bible devotionals, pamphlets that shared the gospel, and practical thoughts on how Christians should treat schooling and government. Katharina also wrote about theology—the study of God. Because she was a woman, that got her into some trouble. But, Katharina wasn't afraid to tell people what she thought. She even rebuked her friend Calvin for executing people who disagreed with his strict moral ideas.

RENEE OF FERRARA (1510-1575), FRANCE / ITALY

Had Renee been born a boy, she would have been King of France. Instead, Renee's third cousin was crowned king and Renee was married to a duke in Italy, the home country of the Roman Catholic Church. She filled her court with Reformed servants, tutors, and ministers and cared for the sick, poor, and orphaned. While Calvin was on the run from France, she took him in just as she took in other French Reformed refugees. They developed a life-long friendship.

Eventually, Renee's Roman Catholic husband realized his wife was helping the Reformation succeed and took away her five children. After his death, Renee

returned to France and helped the Reformed believers there, called the Huguenots. Renee helped save the lives of many believers during the Saint Bartholomew's Day Massacre, when thousands of Reformed citizens were killed.

CHARLOTTE DE BOURBON (C.1546-1582), FRANCE / THE NETHERLANDS

Charlotte de Bourbon's father sent her to a convent when she was young. Somehow, Charlotte learned of salvation in Jesus by grace through faith. By the time Charlotte was eighteen, she ran the convent. Charlotte taught her nuns the truth about the Bible and salvation. When the Church realized Charlotte was teaching Reformed beliefs, she fled to the protection of Prince Frederick III in Germany.

Prince William of Orange also visited Prince Frederick, looking for soldiers to help him fight a bitter war against the Roman Catholic king of Spain. William wanted the

Reformed Church in the Netherlands—now Holland and Belgium—to be free to worship. Charlotte married William and homeschooled their six daughters and eight step-children and nephews and nieces, teaching them the Good News of Jesus. Charlotte saved William's life, caring for him day and night for nearly a month after someone tried to murder him for his faith.

HEIDELBERG CATECHISM BY ZACHARIUS URSINUS AND CASPAR OLEVIANUS (1563)

Question: Are all men, then, saved by Christ just as they perished through Adam? Answer: No. Only those are saved who by a true faith are grafted into Christ and accept all His benefits.

That is the twentieth question in the Heidelberg Catechism. There are Bible verses to memorize as well. Martin Luther wrote the first catechism—questions and answers about the Bible—to help children and adults learn what the Bible says about important issues. Catechisms often address common heresies or false teachings during the time they are written.

Prince Frederick III asked the leaders of the Reformed Church for a new catechism that could be used in schools and to help educate pastors. With 126 questions and answers, the Heidelberg Catechism was divided into fifty-two Lord's Day sections so it could be learned in a year. The Catechism is still used in Reformed churches around the world today.

SOLI DEO GLORIA

Once your life has been forever changed by Jesus, you cannot help but live differently. It is not good living that makes Jesus love us. But when we love Jesus, we live good lives for him because we are so grateful for how he loves us. Christians desire to worship and praise God the way he wants to be adored.

The last slogan the Reformers used to help us remember the truth is soli Deo gloria, which means to the glory of God alone. When we glorify someone, we worship and praise them. God is the only one we should glorify. In fact, we should glorify him in everything we do.

What does that mean, exactly? Well, even your schoolwork or sweeping the floor can be done to the glory of God if you do it well for him. You can do all things with an attitude of gratefulness for all that God has done for you. Ephesians 2:10 says: "For we are his workmanship, created in Christ Jesus for good works, which God prepared beforehand, that we should walk in them." God planned good works for each believer before the world even began.

One of the reasons the Reformation happened is Church officials were not living for Jesus the way the Bible tells us to. The Reformers took glorifying God seriously. They wanted Christians to live for Jesus in a way that would honor him. They did not want the Protestant Church to tolerate sin and corruption amongst Christians.

Proper worship glorifies God in the way he tells us he wants to be honored. Scripture clearly says we should worship God alone. Instead, churches were filled with statues of dead Christians.

People prayed to these dead saints and took long trips to visit relics—bones, cloth, and other trinkets that may have belonged to saints. During the Reformation, the statues and relics of saints were thrown out of churches and burned.

Pastors made an effort to hold church services that were simple and focused on teaching Scripture in the language of the people so they could understand what was being said. In the early Reformation the Bible was preached secretly in fields, but by the late Reformation pastors stood at pulpits teaching what the Bible says.

Not only was the Bible taught in churches across Europe, the Reformers also made sure the whole worship service was centered on Scripture and obeyed what the Bible says about worshiping God. A Reformed worship service included Scripture readings, prayers based on what the Bible says, singing Scripture, and the preaching of God's Word. Everything was arranged to glorify God.

In 1 Corinthians 10:31, Paul tells us: "So, whether you eat or drink, or whatever you do, do all to the glory of God." The Bible tells us a lot of things about who God is and how we can glorify him. When you read Scripture, you will want to look for the things God tells

us about himself. Think about how you can glorify him in your own life. Here are some things the Bible tells us about God:

God created all things, including you. We can praise him for his creation.

God is holy. He is set apart from everyone else. He never sins and is never wrong. We can show our love for God by avoiding sinful behaviors.

God is sovereign. He is the King of all events, people, and nations. We can trust him to rule justly.

The Bible tells us other things about God. He is just, wise, loving, good, and truthful. If we love and follow Jesus, God adopts us as his very own children and he becomes our Father. That's such good news. It is something we should praise and thank God for every day, because our thanksgiving brings God glory.

That's really what the Reformation was all about. It was a movement to remember that God is glorious. He is awesome. We are his children, and our job is to glorify him—not ourselves, the Church, or the people who lived before us.

We glorify God by reading his words to us in the Bible and by living out his commands for followers of Jesus. When you remember that salvation is from Jesus alone, by grace alone through faith alone, and that there is nothing good you can do to add to your salvation, that brings God glory.

Just before he ascends to heaven after he rises from the dead, Jesus tells us: "All authority in heaven and on earth has been given to me. Go therefore and make disciples of all nations, baptizing them in the name of the Father and of the Son and of the Holy Spirit, teaching them to observe all that I have commanded you. And behold, I am with you always, to the end of the age." (Matthew 28:18b-20)

As you tell your friends and family about Jesus' sacrifice for their sins, you bring God glory too.

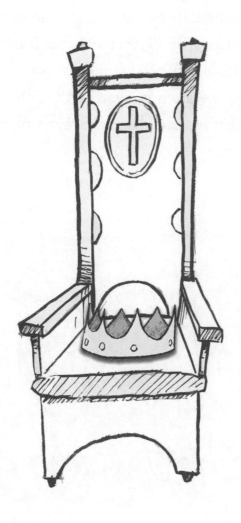

CANONS OF DORT BY SYNOD OF DORT (1619)

The Synod of Dort, with eighty-four Reformed pastors and theologians from the Netherlands, Scotland, England, Germany, Switzerland, and France, was the biggest gathering of scholars during the Reformation. They came together to respond to the teachings of Netherlands professor Jacob Arminius (1560-1609). Arminius was teaching students that we are not saved by the grace of God alone, but that we can choose to reject or to follow God on our own.

The Canons of Dort are five rules known as TULIP. Total Depravity means we are dead in our sins and cannot save ourselves. Unconditional Election means God does not choose to save his people because of anything they do. Limited Atonement means Jesus died for his chosen children. Irresistible Grace means that once God calls you to faith through the Holy Spirit, you will be saved. Perseverance of the Saints means once God saves you, you will follow him for all eternity.

REFORMATION
GOING FORWARD

God worked through the lives of individual Reformers to remind people of the importance of his Word and to bring people to himself through the Good News of Jesus. His people wanted to look more like the early Church in Scripture, and less like the Roman Catholic Church structure with all its extra teachings.

The word Protestant comes from protest— Reformed believers protested the abuses and false

teachings of the Roman Catholic Church. Throughout the Reformation there were wars and persecution—thousands of people died for their faith. By 1648, Europeans agreed to tolerate and accept the beliefs of others. This allowed Christians to separate into groups—or denominations—by beliefs.

While Protestants all held to the five solas, differences in doctrine separated them. Lutherans held to the teachings of Martin Luther, while the Reformed Church followed the writings of John Calvin. The Anglican Church in England and the Presbyterian Church in Scotland disagreed over how to structure leadership and how worship services should proceed. As the Reformation marched onward, new groups of believers began to emerge.

ANABAPTISTS

In 1525, while Ulrich Zwingli was teaching sola Scriptura in Zurich, a group of men in Switzerland felt the Church should be under the authority of the Holy Spirit, rather than under the authority of God's Word. They believed the Holy Spirit speaks directly to and through all believers today. To them, that meant there should be no church leadership. They also believed the church should be separate from government leadership, a radical idea at the time.

This group became known for their insistence that the Bible teaches a believer's baptism of confessing adults. Both Roman Catholics and Reformed believers baptized babies, so they mocked the new group by calling them Anabaptists, or re-baptizers. Anabaptists were frequently burned at the stake or drowned.

The Anabaptist movement went underground, but it spread quickly since every newly baptized believer was declared to be both a priest and a missionary. Anabaptists taught love, modest living, and non-violence, but there were members who believed they were hearing other things from God. Radical Anabaptists caused riots and even war. Today, the Anabaptist movement includes a number of modern-day groups you may recognize, like the Mennonites, Amish, and Quakers.

BAPTISTS

After Bloody Mary killed more than 300 Protestants, Elizabeth became the head of the Church of England. Elizabeth's Church of England was still too close to Roman Catholicism for many Reformed believers, who called themselves Separatists. Many of the Separatists took their families and moved to the Netherlands where William of Orange won religious freedom for his people.

When John Smythe moved his Separatist church to Amsterdam in 1608, he rented a meeting room from an Anabaptist man. Smythe decided the Anabaptists were correct about the baptism of believers and re-baptized himself and about forty of his followers. From there, Smythe's congregation—now called Baptists—spread out. Some traveled back to England while others journeyed to the New World, which we now call the United States of America.

Baptists teach Jesus is the head of the Church—so every congregation makes its own decisions. They also believe every Baptist should share the Good News of Jesus. Those two ideas helped the Church spread quickly. In American, large congregations of African Americans—both slave and free—appreciated

the freedom to praise God while keeping their own cultural ways of worshiping through song and dance. At first, black churches were illegal in some states, but the gospel of Jesus cannot be kept from his people.

PURITANS

Like Baptists, Puritans also began as English Separatists. They felt the Church of England was still too close to the Roman Catholic Church in its beliefs and practices. Because of their desire to purify the Church, people called them Puritans.

Puritans were highly educated, and they emphasized the study of God's Word and prayer. Church services on the Lord's Day could last at least three hours and families

held private worship services in their homes every day of the week. Both men and women were expected to show self-control by waking early in the morning for private Bible study and prayer. In addition to a heavy emphasis on sola Scriptura, Puritans lived their lives soli Deo gloria—to the glory of God alone. They worked hard to care for the sick, widowed, and poor.

One group of Puritans remained in England to work on purifying the Anglican Church. A second group decided the Church of England could never be purified, and they set out for the New World on the Mayflower in 1620. American Puritans welcomed Native Americans and African Americans to their services. Everyone was welcome to serve King Jesus.

Reformed believers have changed the world for Jesus. Today, millions of Christians still live by the slogans Reformers created to remind believers why the Reformation happened in the first place—sola Scriptura, solus Christus, sola gratia, sola fide, and soli Deo gloria.

WESTMINSTER CONFESSION OF FAITH (1646)

Just five years before the close of the Reformation, English King Charles I tried to force the Scottish Presbyterians—a church run by pastors and elders—to accept the Episcopal system which recognized the King as the head of bishops. This helped lead to the English Civil War. The Scots joined the winning side in the war. As a result, the Episcopal system was temporarily abolished, and 151 leaders from Scotland

and England gathered to create a Reformed statement of faith.

The Confession strongly supported sola Scriptura, teaching the Bible is the inspired, inerrant, sufficient, authoritative, clear, and necessary Word of God. It also taught sola gratia—we are saved by God's grace alone. It affirmed the Reformed teaching that God's people are chosen by him in advance—predestined. God is sovereign over all things, but people have responsibility and consequences for their own choices. The Westminster Confession of Faith was an important unifying document for the Reformed Church throughout the world.

TIMELINE

1150

Peter Lombard establishes seven sacraments in the Sentences.

1215

The Fourth Lateran Council under Pope Innocent III changes the Church through hundreds of decrees.

1229

The Synod of Toulouse forbids common people to have Bibles.

1382

John Wycliffe translates the New Testament into English and preaches sola Scriptura.

1398

Jan Hus preaches sola Scriptura in Prague.

1403

The Roman Catholic Church bans many of John Wycliffe's writings.

1415

Hus is burned at the stake as a heretic.

1453

Muslim Turks capture Constantinople.

1455

The Gutenberg Bible is the first major book produced by the printing press.

1478

The Spanish Inquisition begins. Anyone not converted to the Roman Catholic Church is tortured or killed.

1492

Muslims and Jews are thrown out of Spain.

1497

Girolamo Savonarola preaches against Church corruption in Florence and creates the bonfire of the vanities.

1498

Savonarola is burned at the stake.

1501

The Roman Catholic Pope orders the burning of all books that do not support the teaching of the Church.

1517

Martin Luther posts the Ninety-Five Theses to the door of the Wittenberg Castle Church in Germany. The Reformation truly begins.

Philip Melanchthon begins teaching Greek at the University of Wittenberg and becomes good friends with Luther.

1521

Luther is declared a heretic at the Diet of Worms.

1522

Luther finishes the German translation of the New Testament.

1524

The New Testament is translated into Danish.

1525

Tyndale publishes the New Testament in English.

Reformation begins in Poland.

Zwingli bans the Roman Catholic Mass in Zurich.

Katharina Zell directs a relief program for 3,000 refugees fleeing the German Peasants' War.

Anabaptists meet outside Swiss village to baptize each other for the first time.

1527

Sweden becomes Reformed.

Anabaptist Reformers Felix Manz and Michael Sattler martyred for teaching the doctrine of adult baptism.

1528

Reformation begins in Scotland.

1529

Luther and Zwingli meet to argue about Communion. They do not agree.

1533

John Calvin begins the Reformation in France and flees through a window.

King Henry VIII of England divorces his first wife Catherine, the mother of Mary.

1534

Luther completes the German Old Testament.

In France, posters against the mass are erected in the Affair of the Placards. Hundreds are arrested and a dozen or more are killed.

The Church of England separates from the Roman Catholic Church. The king becomes head of the Church.

1536

Reformation begins in Denmark and Norway.

Tyndale is burned at the stake.

Calvin publishes the first edition of Institutes of Christian Religion.

The English Parliament declares the authority of the pope void.

1538

Shrines and relics are destroyed in England.

1540

The New Testament is translated into Icelandic.

Catholics form the Jesuits, a monastic order devoted to education and missions. Catholicism spreads through central and west Africa, parts of Asia, and Brazil.

1541

Calvin returns to Geneva to preach for the remainder of his life.

1544

Princess Renee/Duchess Renee of Ferrara, a Protestant, is imprisoned. Her daughters sent to a convent.

1545

The Roman Catholic Church convenes the Council of Trent to respond to the Protestant Reformation and to discuss Catholic reform. Meets off and on until 1563.

1546

George Wishart of Scotland killed for his faith. In retaliation, Protestants overthrow St. Andrew's Castle, kill Cardinal David Beaton, and make John Knox their preacher.

1547

England further reforms the church under nine-year-old king Edward VI.

John Knox and rebels captured and sentenced as galley slaves for France. Freed nineteen months later.

1549

Calvin and Zwingli agree on the Lord's Supper.

Thomas Cranmer publishes the first edition of the Book of Common Prayer.

Heinrich Bullinger, Zwingli's successor, begins writing The Decades, theology for pastors. He finishes in 1552.

1553

Mary, a Catholic, becomes Queen of England. She kills over 300 Protestants in her five-year reign.

1555

Knox returns to Scotland from his exile in Geneva.

1556

Cranmer burned at the stake.

1558

Knox' The First Blast of the Trumpet Against the Monstrous Regimen of Women published.

Elizabeth becomes Queen of England and allows freedom of worship.

1560

Puritanism begins in England.

France promises the Huguenots freedom of worship.

1562

1,200 French Huguenots are massacred.

1563

John Foxe's Book of Martyrs published.

The Heidelberg Catechism published.

1566

Heinrich Bullinger writes Second Helvetian Confession to reconcile Calvin and Zwingli's teachings.

1568

The Bible is translated into Czech.

Civil war begins in the Netherlands between Roman Catholics with Spain fighting for them, and Protestants. 18,000 die in the initial fight of a twelve-year war.

1572

The St. Bartholomew's Day Massacre begins the open killing of French Huguenots. In the end, the dead number between 30,000 to 100,000.

1575

Charlotte de Bourbon marries William of Orange.

1581

Protestants in the northern Netherlands win independence. Dutch Reformed believers spread across the world.

1598

French Huguenots are granted the freedom to worship in the Edict of Nantes.

1609

John Smythe leads early Baptist Church in the Netherlands.

1610

Arminius' followers state five theological points in the Remonstrance of 1610.

1611

King James publishes the Authorized Version of the Holy Bible.

1618

Protestant rebels in Prague throw government officials out a window into a manure pile. This act begins the Thirty Years' War, in which Protestants and Catholics fight throughout Europe. Over eight million people die.

1619

The Synod of Dort in the Netherlands publishes the Canons of Dort in response to the Remonstrance of 1610.

1620

Puritan Pilgrims sail for the New World. They agree to build a Reformed colony for God's glory.

1638

Reformed Baptists form a church that follows Calvinism and practices believer's baptism.

1646

The Westminster Assembly accepts the Westminster Confession of Faith.

1647

Shorter Westminster Catechism published.

1648

The Reformation ends with the Peace of Westphalia, which ends the Thirty Years' War. Individuals are allowed to worship without fear of persecution.

Larger Westminster Catechism published.

WORKS CONSULTED

Bainton, Roland H. The Reformation of the Sixteenth Century. Beacon Press, 1952, pp. 3-76.

Barrett, Matthew. "The Crux of Genuine Reform." Reformation Theology: A Systematic Summary, edited by Matthew Barrett. Crossway, 2017, pp. 43-63.

Beckwith, Roger. (1995). "Unmatched Masterpiece." Christian History, Issue 48.

Bray, Gerald. "Late-Medieval Theology." Reformation Theology: A Systematic Summary, edited by Matthew Barrett. Crossway, 2017, pp. 67-110.

Canadian Reformed Theological Seminary. "History." Heidelberg Catechism. heidelberg-catechism.com/en/history. Accessed June 10, 2020.

Curtis, A. Kenneth, J. Stephen Lang, and Randy Petersen. The 100 Most Important Events in Christian History. Revell, 1991, pp. 80-81, 86-121.

Dowley, Tim. Atlas of the European Reformations. Fortress Press, 2015.

Dowley, Tim, editor. Introduction to The History of Christianity: Second Edition. Fortress Press, 2013, pp. 318-327.

Duffy, Eamon. Saints and Sinners: A History of the Popes. Yale University Press, 2006, pp. 177-208.

Durant, Will. The Reformation. Simon & Schuster, 1957, pp. 293-402.

Editors. (1985). "A People Called Baptist." Christian History, Issue 6. Christianhistoryinstitute.org/magazine/article/people-called-baptist. Available June 10, 2020.

Editors. (Reprint). "1536: John Calvin Publishes Institutes of the Christian Religion." Christian History, Issue 28, pp. 38-39.

Editors. (1986). "John Calvin: Did You Know?" Christian History, Issue 12, pp. 5.

Editors. (1985). "The Anabaptists: Did You Know?" Christian History, Issue 5. Christianhistoryinstitute.org/magazine/article/anabaptists-did-you-know. Available June 10, 2020.

Editors. (1995). "Thomas Cranmer and the English Reformation: Did You Know?" Christian History, Issue 48, pp. 5.

Editors. (1986). "T.U.L.I.P." Christian History, Issue 12, pp. 25.

Editors. (1987). "William Tyndale: Did You Know?" Christian History, Issue 16, pp. 5.

Chadwick, Harold J. "Introduction to John Foxe and His Book." Foxe's Book of Martyrs. Bridge-Logos, 2001, pp. vii-x.

Grant, George and Wilbur, Gregory. The Christian Almanac. Cumberland House, 2004.

Grun, Bernard. The Timetables of History. Simon & Schuster, 1963.

"Heidelberg Catechism." Western Theological Seminary. students.wts.edu/resources/creeds/heidelberg.html. Accessed June 10, 2020.

Horton, Michael. "What are We Celebrating? Taking Stock after Five Centuries." Reformation Theology: A Systematic Summary, edited by Matthew Barrett. Crossway, 2017, pp. 13-35.

Hyde, Rev. Daniel R. "A Brief Introduction on the Nature of History of the Canons of Dort." Westminster Seminary California. wscal.edu/about-wsc/doctrinal-standards/canons-of-dort. Accessed June 9, 2020.

Klaassen. (1985). "A Fire That Spread Anabaptist Beginnings." Christian History, Issue 5. Christianhistoryinstitute.org/ magazine/article/anabaptist-beginnings. Available June 10, 2020.

Maas, Korey D. "Justification by Faith Alone." Reformation Theology: A Systematic Summary, edited by Matthew Barrett. Crossway, 2017, pp. 511-547.

MacGregor, Jerry and Marie Prys. 1001 Surprising Things You Should Know about Christianity. Baker Books, 2002, pp. 28, 42, 61-62, 64-65, 83-94, 105-108.

Miller, Kevin Dale. (1995). "John Knox: Did You Know?" Christian History, Issue 46, pp. 5.

Niemczyk, Cassandra. (1994). "The American Puritans: Did You Know?" Christian History, Issue 41. Christianhistoryinstitute. org/magazine/article/American-puritans-did-you-know. Available June 10, 2020.

Niemczyk, Cassandra. (1994). "The Baptists: Did You Know?" Christian History, Issue 6. Christianhistoryinstitute.org/ magazine/article/Baptists-did-you-know. Available June 10, 2020.

Norwich, John Julius. Absolute Monarchs: A History of the Papacy. Random House, 2011, pp. 275-298.

O'Malley, John W., SJ. A History of the Popes: From Peter to the Present. Rowman & Littlefield Publishers, Inc., 2010, pp. 171-187.

"Peter Lombard." Theopedia. Theopedia.com/peter-lombard. June 1, 2020.

Tait, Edwin Woodruff. (2015). "Westminster Confession of

Faith." Christian History, Issue 25. christianhistoryinstitute. org/magazine/article/westminster-confession-of-faith. Accessed June 10, 2020.

Thompson, Mark D. "Sola Scriptura." Reformation Theology: A Systematic Summary, edited by Matthew Barrett. Crossway, 2017, pp. 145-187.

Trafton, Jennifer and Leland Ryken. (2006). "Richard Baxter and the English Puritans: Did You Know?" Christian History, Issue 89. Christianhistoryinstitute.org/magazine/article/ Richard-baxter-and-the-english-puritans-did-you-know. Available June 10, 2020.

Trueman, Carl R. and Eunjin Kim. "The Reformers and Their Reformations." Reformation Theology: A Systematic Summary, edited by Matthew Barrett, Crossway, 2017, pp. 111-141.

Tucker, Ruth. Parade of Faith: A Biographical History of the Christian Church. Zondervan, 2011, pp. 197-335.

VanDoodewaard, Rebecca. Reformation Women: Sixteenth-Century Figures Who Shaped Christianity's Rebirth. Reformation Heritage Books, 2017, pp. 15-24, 63-70, 91-98.

Christian Focus Publications publishes books for adults and children under its four main imprints: Christian Focus, CF4K, Mentor and Christian Heritage. Our books reflect our conviction that God's Word is reliable and Jesus is the way to know him, and live for ever with him.

Our children's publication list covers pre-school to early teens. We also publish personal and family devotional titles, biographies and inspirational stories that children will love.

From pre-school board books to teenage apologetics, we have it covered!

Christian Focus Publications Ltd,
Geanies House, Fearn, Ross-shire,
IV20 1TW, Scotland,
United Kingdom.
www.christianfocus.com